#LMAO

Laughing My A_ _ Off!

A collection of humor essays

to help you Lose Weight!

Sunny Brown

For Billy, Locke, and Carlyle.

CONTENTS

ACKNOWLEDGMENTS

I wish to extend my heartfelt gratitude to Joe O'Donnell, Robin Richeson Colter, and the entire talented, and glamorous, team at *B-Metro Magazine*. Special thanks to Joe, also, for your generosity in giving me the opportunity of a lifetime by offering me a monthly column in such a beautiful magazine, for the chance to discover that I was a writer, and for the time and encouragement to find my voice-you changed my life.

Loving thanks goes to Carlyle Brown for her additional editing and her infinite patience.

Thanks and appreciation to everyone who takes the time to read my column and let me know how much you laughed, or how it touched you in some way.

I send all of my love to my children, Locke and Carlyle, who give me so much fun material to write about. You are my inspiration, and my life.

And, gratitude, always, to my mother, Mary Conklin, for being such an inspiration, and offering us your unwavering support in every way.

And, of course, to my husband, Billy, who always makes me laugh, and for without whom none of this would be possible. I thank you for... Everything.

INTRODUCTION

Back in 2011 I was given the opportunity to write my own monthly column in *B-Metro Magazine*, a new publication that was being launched. The essays in this book are some of my reader's favorites from that column.

I feel that laughter is a gift we get to share. I hope that I have given you that gift in this book. Thank you for spending some of your valuable time here with me.

With all my gratitude,
Sunny

THE VIRTUAL EMPTY NEST

I am sitting here in my newly empty nest. My last child has bailed out of the family home and spread her wings and flown off to college, literally. I just can't quite figure out how those eighteen years flew by so fast. It's been quite an adjustment. I've been through something similar to this before when my first child left for college. I would go sit in his room in his Lazy-Boy recliner and cry. The worst of it came when his birthday rolled around and it was the first time he wasn't home for us to celebrate it together. So I baked him his favorite cake and actually shipped it to him, overnight, to California, where he is in school. My husband said it was the most expensive birthday cake ever, and that I couldn't do it again. Ever.

I'm glad my daughter has a summer birthday.

So, here I am experiencing all those feelings of change again, but this time there is not another child at home to keep me from sinking into a state of depression by demanding my attention (hubby doesn't count), just an old dog, an older cat, and an ancient tortoise. Maybe I better go find the Prozac.

No! I decided that I must make a plan to keep myself busy, you know, create a new life for myself for, oh, I don't know, the next forty-five years! That's a long time. So, I began to imagine all the possibilities of what I could do, and the more I thought about it, the more excited I became I mean, I can do anything now. I can act and do and behave and dress any way I want to now, and not worry about embarrassing anyone (hubby doesn't count this time either-he willingly married into it).

For starters, to cheer myself up I started going through some recent photos of my birthday party and posted some of them on my Facebook page. In no time at all I got a message from my daughter demanding to know what in the world I am doing posting those photos? That I look drunk. Then, I got another one from my son asking why I was drunk and why would I post those photos? I also got a message from my mother asking if I have turned to drinking now that I am an empty nester? I just thought they were fun, but I took them down. So much for my freedom.

I never really had time to watch much television before, so I thought I might get caught up on some shows that I had missed, like SMASH! So, as I settled in to watch it, I tweeted that it was time to get SMASHED! And within seconds my daughter was texting me asking if I realize what that meant and how it made me sound? Her friends were following me on twitter, she said, and had re-tweeted it to her. I told her to tell her friends to stop stalking me, that I don't follow them.

When I posted a new photo on Instagram of a picture that my husband had taken of me, my son immediately texted me and said he saw it, and then a tense silence followed. When I asked him what he thought of it, he asked me what was he supposed to think about it, what with me dressed like that. I guess he doesn't like my left shoulder. That was the only thing showing except for my face, so I am hoping that was the part he objected to. But, you never know with kids.

Forget Big Brother watching, it's the Big Kids you

have to worry about. My kids are stalking my every move. The NSA could call them for info. It feels like I am under constant surveillance. If I post a comment or make a tweet late at night, they immediately want to know what's wrong, why am I up so late? If it is a photo of me having a good time, they want to know if I am drinking.

If you have tried, as I have, to gain some independence from your kids and tried desperately to cut the cord, I have news for you, it's wireless now! They may be saying, "Look Mom, No Hands!" but they can get to you from anywhere, making it feel like they have their hands, firmly clasped around yours. I can't get away. If I check in on foursquare they tell me that it is no place for me to be, aren't I too old for that crowd? I thought college was supposed to be a hands free experience, a time when they were on their own, and left you on your own, too. But, with their phones and surveillance equipment, I mean- tech tools, it's anything but hands off. And now, with Facetime and Skyping, I can even see and hear the disbelief on their faces to go along with the tone of their texts. It's unnerving.

Maybe they weren't expecting me to embrace my newly found independence so quickly. Maybe they thought I would just sit around in the dark, crying, lying in their beds, feeling like my life was over. Maybe I thought so, too. And I did do that for about a week. Maybe to them it seems as if I have adapted and am having too much fun. Maybe I have and maybe I am! My kids should be enjoying their lives and having as much fun as I am. After all, they couldn't wait to get out on their own. They spent years telling me they couldn't wait for college, and if I asked where they were heading anytime they were walking out the door, they accused me of being too involved in their lives. Now, I would say the roles have reversed.

That's the problem with today's wireless technology; my kids might not be physically here with me, but they are ever present in my daily life. In reality, I kind of like it that way. Just don't tweet that I said that.

THE PAIN OF UNREQUITED LOVE

Love hurts when you're in love with a heel. While we usually celebrate the joys of being in love, I am sure there are plenty of people out there who can relate to the pain of not having a love reciprocated. It happened to me, and I want to share the story with you in the hopes that it will help prevent you from following in my footsteps.

I fell head over heels in love one time, but the feeling was not returned. I was young, out on my own for the first time and looking for love in all the wrong places, when I suddenly caught a glimpse of the object of my affection and I just "knew" right then and there, that we would be a perfect pair. It was love at first sight for me. I was vulnerable and easily seduced by flirty promises of fun evenings on the town spent dancing the night away, strolls through the city, lunch dates and window-shopping. It was all pure romantic fantasy and I easily bought into it. Like many other young girls inexperienced in making such important decisions, I ignored early warning signs that this relationship was not a good fit. Whenever we were together, I was in heaven, and I truly believed we would be together forever. I even made room in my closet!

It was great, in the beginning. Each time we stepped out I felt like I was floating on air, as if my feet weren't even touching the ground. And then, suddenly, it would all change, and I would be left sitting there slumped and dejected. But I continued to ignore the pain, the betrayals. All the nights taken out dancing that ended with tears in my eyes while I watched everyone else having fun. But we looked so good together. I admit that I was guilty of feeling smug, and enjoyed showing off when we went out, like I had won a prize. People even commented on what a perfect pair we were. So I continued to hide behind the image. We looked the part, but it was all an illusion. The truth was, there was no foundation, no sole, and it hurt.

But, stubbornly, I continued to endure the pain in silence, choosing to go out in the evenings over and over, only to be left, again and again, sitting on the bench while my friends (much more sensible than I) enjoyed dancing the night away, or running through the park, or long afternoon strolls.

I really tried my best to make it work; I tried compromising, shifting my position and expectations I offered unconditional love. But, it was not reciprocated. Unconditional love never betrays. It can always be counted on; like my favorite pair of jeans. They never tell me that I've gained too much weight they just stretch or expand somehow, always a perfect fit, accommodating my needs, lying if they must to spare my feelings. But no matter what I did to try and fix the situation I was just left swollen from pain and tears, and shame. Shame that I had hidden for so long the price that I had paid for this form of abuse.

Then, one day, something different, the complete opposite of my current love, caught my eye, and this time I could tell it would be the real thing. So, I decided to take a chance and try my luck.

This was a sensible relationship from the very start,

beginning with where I first caught a glimpse, in a sensible store when I was out shopping, not some fancy, high-end shop full of pretenders. This relationship wasn't built on the high of imagined thrills, but grounded in reality. There were no tears, just the joy of being part of the fun again. We really were the perfect pair, and it was unconditional, and this time the feeling was reciprocated. Whatever I wanted to do was immediately met with ease and comfort. There was no pain to try and bandage so that no one would see that we didn't belong together.

I was finally happy, and I knew it was time for me to send my old love packing for good. I was afraid that I would slip back into that uncomfortable relationship if I let it hang around. So, I boxed up those beautiful 4 1/2" red and white polka dot Stuart Weitzman stilettos and donated them, hoping that another girl would be a better fit, and they would find a lifetime of happiness together.

And I have been so happy in love with my flats ever since. No more pretending for the sake of looks or image. I'm older now, and wiser. Life is short, and it's okay if I'm a little shorter, too. I still fall hard when I see a beautiful pair of stilettos, but, after all, it doesn't hurt to look! As the saying goes, "If the shoe fits, wear it!" But that's the key; it must be a good fit. Being in love with the *wrong* pair of shoes is like being in love with the wrong guy, it hurts when you're in love with a heel.

THE DARK SIDE

I have fallen madly in love all over again. It's all I can think about, as it always happens when you are in the throws of new love. I'm not sure if it is real love or just lust, but either way, I'm consumed by it. Although this isn't my first time, it feels like the first time whenever I surrender myself to pleasure; stealing a glimpse, the tingling sensation of anticipation when I'm ever so slowly removing all the outer layers that lie between me and my fulfillment. I know I shouldn't be doing this, that it's wrong and not a healthy relationship-- especially when I become obsessed and overindulge. I had made promises to people that I care about that I wouldn't let this happen again, and now, in some moment of weakness I gave in.

I really do feel bad that I am cheating. Cheating on myself most of all, sneaking around trying not to get caught, like a thief in the night. Creating all kinds of secret hiding places to sneak off and enjoy a quick nibble or even just to inhale a whiff of the intoxicating scent that brings a rush of excitement through my entire body. I know I am particularly weak and vulnerable for a late afternoon delight. I actually feel myself trembling with anticipation for the moment when I will be able to sneak away and finally be able to satiate my desire. I thought that I had become very clever with my hiding places all around the house, in my closet, in my car, anywhere I can have an undisturbed moment to myself, and even in my purse. And then the panic sets in; I start thinking I've heard someone, and that I will be caught. And then the wild frenzy to try and hide my indiscretion and pretend every thing is normal. I give a feeble attempt at pretending that I was just coming out of the kitchen, office, or bedroom looking for something, my face flushed, my breath giving me away, and my hands trembling with fear, shame, and embarrassment, trying to wipe away any tell-tell signs of my indiscretion. When, in fact, I know, and they know, and I know that they know that I know, that I was really giving in to the dark side of myself.

And then, that feeling of regret that sets in immediately afterwards, well, not immediately, I do enjoy the aftertaste that lingers on the lips and breath for a few precious moments after such a pleasurable experience. And then, as I come crashing down from that sugar high, as I invariably do, I must have it yet again, and I begin hungrily licking my fingers to see if there is any hint left, any taste of the decadence left behind. I am addicted to it like a lover, and I must have it! I can't live without it, not even for one day.

I know myself, and I know that too often I have a tendency to go all the way, to carry things too far, not knowing when to stop. Passion can be a scary emotion, making you feel things intensely, and I will tell you, I am passionate for the sensuous, warm sensation melting in my mouth and sliding ever so slowly down my throat. It's not for everyone, but I find it gives me the most pleasure.

Whatever some people might think of my other vices, I have always had good taste in this respect. Even my husband respects me for this. But, it costs you. This is not a cheap love affair. You get what you pay for, always.

There is no faking it with me. I can't get into cheap substitutions, tacky plastic wrapping, or waxy milk chocolate. Only the sinful decadence of very dark chocolate does it for me. And I am willing to pay an obscene amount for it. I am embarrassed by how much I am willing to hand over to enjoy myself.

Of course, there is always a price to be paid for one's guilty pleasures. And that time has come for me. I must face up to what this fooling around has cost me-and it's not pretty. It's time to get tough with myself, to take an honest look at what my secret love has done to me. I see it when I look in the mirror, the extra weight I am carrying around from too many late night rendezvous. I lost my self-control, and now it's time to lose something else, it's time to lose those extra pounds that my love of dark chocolate has put upon me, to be held accountable for my actions, and to do something about it. It's all so bitter sweet.

But first, I must figure out what to wear to rid myself of this problem lover. I need a new wardrobe to encourage myself to get on that treadmill. One cannot just throw on any old thing and head out the door. I need to go shopping, especially for shoes, the shoe is the crucial piece to helping you accomplish your goals. It is having the right shoe that will give you the motivation to go for that run, walk, dance, or ZUMBA!

All that pleasure and a new pair of shoes, it's a sweet happy ending, after all.

WALKING LESSONS

It's difficult to write when you are crying. You can't see to type through the swollen, watery eyes, and trying to decipher what you've written after the tears have smudged your words is nearly impossible. But I can't help it, I am listening to the strains of "Pomp and Circumstance" playing through the house, and it gets me every time. It creates a burning desire within me to dust off my clarinet. Which makes everybody else cry.

Every year at this time the music of "Pomp and Circumstance" is played for graduates all over the country. Being in the concert band when I was in high school, I learned and relearned the music every year to play at graduation. Over and over and over and over, we played that slow, steady march for the year's graduates to step up and receive their hard-earned, or much prayed for, diplomas. After my mouth ached and my lips went numb from playing for forty solid minutes, I remember wishing that we could just speed it up really fast and watch them all break out into a run and grab them and go. Actually, I have often wondered why that music is not an upbeat tempo to match the commencement of an exciting new chapter the graduates are about to embark on in their new lives. It just seemed like one more way for them to drag out the school year.

But this year I want them to have to play it for as long as possible. I want the school year to drag on, because, my daughter, my baby, is graduating from high school, and I haven't quite accepted that fact yet. I still have so much to teach her. I am not finished molding her into the person that I want her to be! And we still have so much shopping to do, so many shoes to buy! I felt that I still had so much to teach her before she stepped out on her own two feet for the first time. I kept thinking that I needed some last words of wisdom to pass along. And then it dawned on me that she had already learned all of the important life lessons when she learned to walk in high heels for the first time. Your goal is much the same-to step out into the world on your own two feet and carry yourself through life with grace and confidence. Shoe shopping has so many teachable moments. So, here, in no particular order, are the walking lessons for life that I gave my daughter:

Keep your eyes looking up, but your feet on the ground. Don't worry about falling down, only not getting back up would be your downfall. It's a little wobbly sometimes, trying something new, but eventually you get the hang of it, and find you can even run with the best of them. Invest only in the best. Keep the ones that won't cause you pain and make you cry. Remember, quality over quantity. Put your best foot forward. Sometimes you have to step out of your comfort zone. Sometimes you need a little polishing. Learn to keep your balance. Take it one step at a time. Learn to walk first. Relax, and don't be afraid to kick up your heels. Sometimes you will have big shoes to fill. It's all about Self Confidence! Don't fall in love with a heel. Shatter the glass slipper-ceiling-mirror-no limitations on yourself. Don't believe in "One Size Fits All." Everyone has their own fit in the world. Walk your own path. Put one foot in front of the other. Don't drag your feet. You're bound to get scuff marks. Go barefoot occasionally, you'll need the break. Remember to enjoy the "Free Gifts!"

On her graduation day, my daughter was indeed well prepared for walking across that stage, and into the next one on her life's adventure-after all, she has a great shoe collection.

After writing this, I felt much better. And everyone else did, too, when I decided to turn my clarinet into a lamp.

WHAT LIES BENEATH

I grew up with the understanding that it was what was underneath that counted. That real beauty was not the outer shell we dressed up in and presented to the outside world, as that was a temporary mask, a pretense. No, for real beauty, one must have a solid foundation to hold you up and give you support in times of doubt and temptation, times that might lead you to question your resolve. I was taught that you do not, in fact, "let it all hang out." That if there is a problem that rolls around, a little wrinkle that pops up, that one is to suck it up and carry on. That you don't draw attention to the problem, you seek to minimize it, and just because we try to downplay our trouble spots and not hold them up to the light for the world to see, does not mean we are lying to ourselves, it just means we are presenting another view, an alternate angle of the same view.

What we have hidden just below the outer layer of dressing shapes and mold our perceptions, of who we perceive ourselves to be and how others see us. It is crucial then to have a firm control of our less desirable traits, to keep them in check and hidden so they do not inadvertently bump into view, creating a distorted and undesirable vision that is not consistent with how we wish to be seen. It is not about concealing truth, but it is not about a false reality, either. It is about keeping things under control. I have been accused of being a control freak, but in my own defense, I will say that whatever lies are beneath my outer surface, will remain out of sight. Control starts at the top, and comes in mighty handy against the daily assault of Snack Attack, Sweet Tooth, Afternoon Slump, and, mostly, Gravity.

Therefore, I give my most deeply grateful thanks for my SPANX. I cannot begin to tell you, and indeed I would not, the countless times that I have entrusted my SPANX to cover my a@% and keep me on the up and up, figuratively speaking. My SPANX are like my most glamorous girlfriends, they know all of my best kept secrets and would never let me down by revealing them. We are inseparable, but they are content to remain out of sight, to stay behind the seams playing a supporting role, lifting me up and letting me enjoy my time in the glamour light. Whenever I have moments of doubt about wearing the newest addition to my Little Black Dress collection, or my favorite sleek slacks, I just have to remember my secret weapon, my SPANX. They are like body guards, working undercover to back me up and make me feel safe and secure in the knowledge that I will be able to smoothly carry on with all of the tasks, appointments, and commitments that I have to meet during the course of the day, with a calm and confident demeanor. This confidence that comes from wearing SPANX is a "must have" accessory, and a every smart girl's hidden asset, one that will inevitably lead to an improvement in your bottom line.

As you peel away the outer layers of artifice, the daily mask we put on to present to the world, SPANX offers a strong support foundation that will allow you to enhance your best features and present yourself to your best advantage.

In gratitude, I have written this little poem:

An Ode to SPANX:

My tummy's flat, my boobs are not,
I look in the mirror and think, "My God, I look hot!"
After the twisting and turning, I've worked up a sweat,
Surely that's a few pounds off, so I rest a bit.
I'm "of a certain age" but you will never know,
Because, thanks to my SPANX
No tell tale lines will ever show.

Looking back, I can see how important this advice has been to me, that underneath it all, you need to have a strong, but flexible foundation to lie back on. Of course, hindsight is 20/20 and thanks to SPANX the view from the rear is looking firmly in control.

ALL BY MY SELFIE
"Wherever you go, there you are." ~ Jon Kabat-Zinn

It's true what they say, that you can run but you cannot hide. And it's especially true that you cannot hide from your self. I know this, because I have been hiding out from myself for the past few days now. But no matter where I go-there I am. It's like I'm stalking myself.

I have given in and come to grips with the fact that I have to live in a world of self-service; sometimes, I even prefer it that way. I can be self-serving if I have to. But, now, I have to take my own pictures, too? Just because I sleep with a photographer doesn't mean I am one.

I mean it was fine at first, if people were interested in seeing the slice of plain, dry toast that I had for breakfast. And, if someone was really dying to know what the mosquito bite looked like on my left ankle, well, who was I to deny them that privilege? I didn't mind, too much, snapping a photo and sharing it with the world.

So, even though it was a struggle to remember, I started trying to keep my phone with me at all times, just so I could share those exciting moments of my day when I am cleaning up the cat's hairball, or doing laundry. It's strange, but I found that life does seem more meaningful when you are sharing your frustrations and photos of the rude driver in front of you with your Instagram followers. And the more likes and comments you get, the more you come to realize that your life *does* matter, and not just to you. In fact, you can't be living life just for your self. Keeping things private is just being selfish. And how would you even know any of it really happened if no one was there to judge it? You have to share your selfies with the rest of us!

Taking selfies, however, is not something you just automatically know how to do. It is a learned skill. You must spend hours in front of the mirror with your phone practicing taking the perfect poses. You must learn what angle to hold your arm, which one is your best side, and how to purse your lips into the perfect fish pucker. I'm sure there is a class you could take to learn how to do it. In any case, you must do it. The world will not be denied knowing the most mundane details of your life, but you must make them look exciting! We want to see how much fun you have brushing your teeth, so add some music to the photos if you have to, but please, don't bore us. And you have to look beautiful, surrounded by gorgeous people, and in a fabulous, tropical location.

I'll admit that it has taken me a while to embrace this selfie idea. I mean, when I am in the middle of enjoying my favorite chocolate, I don't naturally think that I should be taking a picture of myself eating it. When I am dressed up to go enjoy a night out with my husband, I never think about other people not getting to share that moment with me. Maybe it's true that I'm just too self-absorbed. At any rate, in the beginning, it was just kind of annoying to have to remember to take my picture sipping my coffee, and then trying to recreate the moment when I did forget, but I agreed to play along, since this isn't just about me. However, things began to take a nasty turn when I felt myself trying to snap a photo of me during one of my darkest moments-Yes, I took a photo of myself without a hat covering my head. And still two days out from next hair appointment! And I was in bad lighting, too. I couldn't let a photo like that of me get out into public.

After that, it seemed that my right hand really turned on me, lurking around every corner, coming at me relentlessly. The more I protested the more invasive it got, even though I was pleading for it to stop. After the no-hat incident, I began to try and hide from it, but it kept following me everywhere I went, as if it was attached to me or something, always with that phone, threatening to expose what I was wearing to walk the dog, or that I need a manicure. I began to actually be afraid of my right hand. The last straw was when I was just trying to go about my day doing absolutely nothing interesting, and my right hand didn't believe me-it was certain that everyone would want to see me thinking. It was trying to snap my photo. I couldn't get away, I even ran into a fence trying to escape. I am going to have to take out a restraining order against myself. You can go to my Instagram page and see the video for your self. It was all caught on camera. And I shared it with you, because I am being selfless.

Certainly, there are times when it's fun to have my

photo taken, but I don't want to have to do it myself. That's just another reason why it's nice to be married to Papa Razzi. But, sometimes I just want to be left alone- without my selfie.

You can check out Sunny's selfies at instagram.com/itsreallysunny

THE *SOUTHERN LIVING* MAGAZINE CHRISTMAS CAKE

I am in a state of panic! I can't believe the season is already here. I don't believe those people that say it has been happening like this every year since we began keeping time. This year really has gone by faster. It has something to do with Global Warming, I think. Anyway, I'm panicked because it's almost time to make the *Southern Living* Christmas Cake and I haven't even started on all of my other Christmas obligations yet.

Several years ago, as a special mother/daughter bonding experience, my daughter and I decided that we would make the Christmas cake that's on the cover of the *Southern Living* magazine. And so, without any warning, a tradition was born. I know, I can you hear you all

29

laughing from here. And now you know why I am panicked. This cake is a serious undertaking, not something left to the once a year home cook. But, you know, we will do anything, and go to any lengths, to stay in bondage to our children and prove to them that we are just as good of a mom as Jennifer's mom. I mean, how hard could it be, right? They give you all the directions right there.

Well, I found out that the hard part is staying awake, or alive, long enough to finish it. I am thinking that is why they have "Living" in their title; it's some sort of clue. I mean really it is a cake-baking marathon if you wait thirty days to make it. But, I was undaunted!

The first *Southern Living* "I'll See this Cake Done Before I Am" Cake that we made was the "Gift Box" cake. Oh! What a beauty! A three-tiered white cake wrapped with a sparkly, edible red ribbon and big bow on top with gingerbread man cookies decorating the sides. We were so proud! It would be a picture perfect centerpiece for our holiday table at Christmas lunch.

We, actually my daughter, insisted that we agree to make the cake look *exactly* as it looks on the cover; this is very important that you remember this detail. The devil is in the details. I suggest you negotiate this point carefully before deciding to take this on yourself. Since we wanted this to eat for Christmas Day lunch, I decided that we should make it the day before Christmas Eve. That would give us two days, plenty of time. So we opened the magazine, found the recipe and started taking notes on all the ingredients we needed. I got writer's cramp.

Un-deterred we went to the grocery store, which I vowed never to do (right up there on the altar when I said all those other vows) to get the ingredients we needed. As the hours went by, we were finding what we needed, until it came to edible glitter. They didn't have it. Oh, well, we will just stop by one of the other grocery stores on the way home. Three hours and forty-five minutes later we got to the check out and I had to max out my credit card. On the way home we stopped at three more stores to find edible glitter, to no avail. We couldn't find it anywhere. My daughter was very upset. Without it, it wouldn't sparkle and look *just like the picture*. Edible glitter almost ruined our Christmas. And then, in a moment of brief clarity, the spirit of the holidays enlightened me, so I cast off the burden onto Santa Clause by calling my husband and threatening to go all holiday crazy on him if he didn't find it. And, voila, I felt so much better.

Once home, we set up all the ingredients and, let's just say that, two days after Christmas we had a beautiful cake ready to eat. Well, at least it was still Christmas break. And it sparkled. My husband and son loved it, my daughter ate a tiny bite and I never wanted to see it again. We did take a picture.

I thought I would never go in the kitchen again, but, sure enough, the next year rolled around and we saw the cake on the cover of *Southern Living* magazine and my daughter reminded me that we "always" did that, so…I think that was the year of the cake with the angels around it. I can't remember; they all run together now. We did make the Gift Box cake again, one year when it was a coconut cake on the cover because we don't like coconut. My mom's favorite has been the cake that was actually on the cover of the November issue one year, the Pecan Pie Cake.

I naively thought that maybe we wouldn't be so angry, I mean harried, if we made the cake in November instead of December. But this particular cake has so many parts to it, it's like building a house-I needed to start in mid-summer. I actually think they built a new house across the street from us from the ground up in the same amount of time we made this cake. I remember I kept racing them to see which of us would finish first. I think they installed their landscaping, too. The problem was that it had to look *exactly* like the picture. And this particular cake, being a fall cake and all, had these *darling* little "pecans" for a garnish. I want you to remember this, it's very important: It's the garnish that will choke the joy from you, every time. Lest you think they were just a bunch of pecans sprinkled around the cake, you must know they were not. You had to get whole pecans, but shelled, and take some pie dough and wrap partly around the pecans, and brush with a glaze, and bake, to make them look like pecans, because the real things would have just been too plain. The whole thing took a good day and a half. But that's not all! There was also a pile of "leaves" adorning the cake. And, you know by now they were not real leaves; the real ones aren't sparkly, or edible, like the glitter ones are. You had to take cookie dough and cut out leaves and then roll up 300 pieces of aluminum foil in various sizes, drape the dough leaves over the foil balls so that they are "3D" leaves (not flat leaves!), brush with a glaze and bake. That took another week. The cake was finished in time for Christmas, so it worked out. The only problem was that it was so damn heavy I couldn't carry it to the table, and it had to be refrigerated. It took up too much room in the already packed kitchen refrigerator so everybody came down to the basement to look at it inside the downstairs fridge. We served it from there and ate it on the Ping-Pong table.

My personal favorite has been the Chocolate Gingerbread Toffee Cake. It's delicious. It tastes like Christmas! In fact, we made that one the last two years in a row, because I love it so much, and because, I know you won't believe me, but I forgot about it the first year we made it due to the exhaustion from the month it took to construct it. It is another cake that must be refrigerated and it got left in the basement refrigerator and totally forgotten about for two days. I wept when we found it. My daughter did, too. So we made it again last year.

In the event that this story of pure holiday Christmas joy has inspired you to begin your own tradition for making the *Southern Living* Christmas Cake I have some lessons learned that I am willing to pass along as my gift to you, dear reader.

First: Begin saving up your cake baking budget for at

least six months prior to starting on the cake. You may have to leave someone off the Christmas shopping list. I hope it's not yourself.

Secondly: Start getting plenty of rest and mentally preparing for the experience. Since the cake photo will not come out until November the first, you will only have 55 days to make it. You will be in a cake baking frenzy, a haze, an alternate life, until it is done. I advise you to cancel all other holiday commitments until you are finished. Make yourself a note to do them in July.

Thirdly: Make room in your refrigerator for the designated "Cake Space." Do not worry about making room in your pantry for all the left over ingredients- you will never use them again. Yes, I know you only used 1/8 of a teaspoon.

Fourth: If you are making any of these cakes for desert, you will have to have everyone over to your house for the holiday meal. They are so heavy they are not transportable.

And I have a piece of advice for *Southern Living*, too: I think the Christmas cake issue should come wrapped in a brown paper cover.

THE CARD IS IN THE MAIL

Being raised in the South, I was, of course, brought up to have good manners. And I was taught that good manners are always about thinking of others. It's a pearl of wisdom, passed down through the generations. Just like my grandmother's string of pearls, having good manners is one my mother passed down to me and that I am now passing along to my own daughter. But, much like a lot of heirlooms, good manners will become dulled and tarnished if allowed to go unused. My mother really impressed upon me the idea that good manners are an essential accessory that you must have with you every day. I've learned that you really will be in good hands if you're nice to people, and it feels so nice to be in good hands, don't you think?

Think how much more peaceful and harmonious the world would be if we only gave more consideration to others. If it were only that easy. Take the handwritten letter, for instance. A sure sign that you were brought up with good manners and took the time to think of others. I know it can seem like a quaint and charming idea, a relic from the past, left to tarnish like old silver that no one wants to take the time to polish anymore; I mean, who has the time, really? I know I don't. Actually, I know that my mother will polish my silver when she comes to visit for Thanksgiving, and how disappointed she would be if she got here and found that it had already been done. It would make her feel like she wasn't needed, and that would not be very considerate of me, taking away my mother's joy and happiness like that--and at the holidays, too. I know it's what she looks forward to every year, the highlight of her year even. I am certain that Alabama winning the SEC title is a distant second to this. I know this because she always asks me about it when she is planning to come to my house for the holidays. She always calls me and says, "Do I need to bring plastic utensils or are you going to try and make us eat with your tarnished black silver again this year?" That's why it doesn't bother me at all that I never lay eyes on my silver until she comes for Thanksgiving. It plagues her mind, bless her heart. I've even thought about getting her a card to let her know how much I appreciate her polishing my silver.

But that's as far as I've gotten, so I am so glad that it's just the thought that counts. And I have lots of thoughts, many times a day, even; that's just how I am. And sometimes, I even actually do buy the card. I have a whole collection of cards, for any occasion in your life. If you have been feeling under the weather, I have thought of you, and bought you a really funny card. I laughed out loud when I read it. In fact, I couldn't stop laughing, and I just knew you felt so much better, because I know I did just thinking of you. You know that big promotion you got? I heard all about it and went out and bought you the perfect card! I couldn't believe that I found one that was so perfect for you. It even had your name on it! I think I might have even actually addressed it! I know you feel so much better just knowing that I have thought of you, and I have, often. Every time I see the card still lying there on my desk, I think of you. Whenever I find it lodged in between the pages of the book I am reading, I think of you and wonder how you are doing. Every time I accidentally pull it out of my purse when I am trying to find my phone, I curse you; I mean I think of you. Oh, and when I need to send another card that I just bought someone else, but I can't find a stamp, so I have to cut the one off of the envelope with your card in it, I know that you understand, because you are an understanding person--you have good manners, that's why we're friends. I am so glad it's the thought that counts. You are well thought of.

In fact, I think about people all the time. And I really think thoughts about people when I am driving. You wouldn't believe what I thought about the person I saw next to me driving down the road practicing the flute while they were in the driver's seat of their car with the sheet music propped on the steering wheel. But I don't think there is a card for that. Oh, what am I thinking, sure there is. I know driving would be more enjoyable if people would just be more considerate of others and practice using their good manners. I know I became a much more considerate driver when I realized what an important tool hand signals were for communicating your feelings to your fellow drivers. Of course, there are some signals that I just think about but never use, but again, it's the thought that counts, and I feel so much better knowing I thought about it. After all, that's what good manners are for: making you feel so much better.

Oh, I know that I can send a quick, perfunctory "Congrats!" on Facebook, and I can think of you even less than that by just "liking" your status and not even having to form a thought. But it is, after all, the thought that counts, and then too, would I "like" that you have been home sick for a week? And I would only be thinking of you for a brief second, and that is not what good manners is about. When I get you a card I am thinking of you over and over again, sometimes for many months. You are constantly on my mind. So, imagine the surprise I felt when I received a card in the mail from you! I got all excited, because people don't do this anymore, they do not take the time to write a handwritten note on a card, we are the only two people left in the world who do this. That is why we are so close. But, I just can't understand where the time went, I mean you just had that baby; I have a "Congratulations on your new baby girl!" card all ready to send you, it's right here, I see it every day. In fact, I was going to drop it in the mail this afternoon. How can I be receiving an invitation to her wedding? But it was so nice to see your handwriting again, it's lovely, you do have such good manners.

AN ITALIAN LOVE AFFAIR

For some time now I have had the feeling that something is not quite right between my husband and me. I'd had suspicions that he is having an affair of the heart, and then recently found out that he is actually having an Italian love affair with a 29-year-old blonde. She's a sleek and curvy little number named "Sophia". Apparently it was love at first sight when he caught a glimpse of her going down the street. He chased her down and got her number. It seems she was advertising herself like some sort of common streetwalker. He said he became obsessed so he looked her up online and got to know all about her on the Internet. I can't believe I'm even sharing all of this with you, but I suspect there are other women out there, devoted wives and girlfriends who have gone through the same thing.

I first started having my suspicions when I noticed he was spending a lot more time than usual on the computer, but would close the page whenever I came into the room. I would hear him speaking in what sounded like he was learning Italian. I heard him cooing in whispered tones words like "Pirelli", and "Pininfarina". I just couldn't believe it. Then suddenly, he just brought her home one day and said she was part of the family, like some foreign exchange student. Oh, how he babies her. Apparently she has been around the track a few times and has quite a few miles on her, despite her age. And she always needs something, like a spoiled child. She is such high maintenance. For a 29-year-old, she sure does need a lot of upkeep. Already her skin has gotten old and leathery, with a lot of lines and cracks, from being out in the sun all day, I'm sure. And she goes topless, too. It serves her right! But, now, my car has to stay outside in the weather, while "she" gets the protection of the garage.

I admit it, I was bitter when he first brought her home. I could just see her taking all of his time and attention, and our money. I resented him taking her out on warm sunny days showing her off like some kind of trophy wife. And she didn't like me. She's very temperamental and hard to handle, so I am not allowed behind the wheel-under one perhaps, but not behind it. Maybe she's afraid that I would drive her over a cliff, since she is creating our own "Fiscal Cliff." The amount of money he spends on her makes my shoe-spending look like I'm Cinderella--before the shoe fit. Needless to say, we do not get along. She totally destroys my hair whenever I do get to go along for a ride, and she tries her best to burn me up in the hot sun and ruin my skin. The worst is when she throws stuff in my eyes-it feels like she's scratching my eyes out. It's like being in a fight with one of the "Real Housewives". By the way, with global warming an *actual reality*, I wonder, with all that plastic, are they going to melt?

Anyway, I decided that if he could afford to have another woman in his life, more horsepower to him. I decided that, to be fair, every time "Sophia" got something new, I should, too. So when she had to have special treatment oils massaged into her cracked leathery skin-Spa Treatment for me! New paint job for her-Makeover for me! Oh, he is always spending money on her, buying her all these little accessories, so I was starting to warm up to her. I was beginning to like this arrangement. If she gets a new little hood ornament-I get a new bracelet; She gets a new little decorative name plate-I get a nice sparkling something to wear around my neck. And I was really happy when she got new shoes, because she has to get two pair! I do agree with her that a girl's got to have her wheels. And I really do think that my closet should at least be the same size as her garage space. All in all, this arrangement has actually turned out to be pretty nice. I know some of you in this same situation may have your doubts, but bringing another woman into the relationship like this has turned out to prove to be a lot of fun, for both of us.

It's true that she is still a little jealous, so she makes it very difficult to enjoy any romance, with her being too small up front, and no back seat (she is a bit under developed for an Italian woman). And he is still a bit too possessive of her. I blame James Bond for all of this. Make no mistake about it, James is really all about his newest plaything, not Mother and country. All men like to feel they have a bit of Bond in them, hell, who doesn't? Life's all about the journey and we want to enjoy the ride in style.

So, I have come to appreciate "Sophia" for what she means to my husband. I've come to enjoy our little threesome. I just put on my favorite pair of shoes, wrap a scarf around my hair, slip on my largest, darkest movie star sunglasses, and voila! James and me drive off into the sunset. Ciao, Baby!

SOLITARY CONFINEMENT

I love time to be myself. But it can feel like such a guilty pleasure, telling everyone you are sick and they should go away for the weekend so they won't get it-it's for their own good, you are just thinking of them, as *always*. However, the truth is, everyone needs a little time to themselves, time to spend in quiet reflection on life. I really love reflection, well, mine anyway.

But, right after my mother called and asked me if I would consider keeping her dog for her for ten whole days while she was away on her cruise, I immediately felt guilty. For ten whole days, did I mention that?! I felt guilty because my very first reaction was "Hell, no!" I was very thankful that I had let her call immediately go to voicemail.

Now, I must speak in my own defense (no one else is going to). My mother has babied "Princess" and spoiled her so much that she has developed a real attitude problem. And she doesn't like us, especially my husband. She lays on the sofa the whole time she is here and growls at him under her breath. He's afraid to move. And she is old. I am always fearful that she will die while she is under our care and we will have to put her in the freezer until my mom gets back. So, I just couldn't bring myself to say "yes". I just couldn't do it.

But, as I said, I felt guilty. I really should be happy to help out my mom and take care of her dog while she is cruising around the Caribbean in January. And, then a thought came to me; I remembered that my mother lives at the beach and that she has her own pool. And her own hot tub. And how for a whole 10 days no one would be there. Then I thought how much happier we would all be if her dog just stayed home, I mean-how much happier her dog would be if she could stay in her familiar environment. So, a few days later, I called her back. I told her that I would, of course, love to help her out in any way that I could, but really, wouldn't it be better for

"Princess" if I came there and stayed with her and she could be in her own home; it would be less stressful for her. Well, she was so thankful. I must say, that it always pays to help out friends and family whenever they have a beach house.

I haven't been alone for more than five hours since 1984. I tried not to seem too ecstatic even though I had my bags all packed the week before. I had made plans, BIG plans! Not only was I going to take long walks on the beach, write, make peace with my mother, and completely plan out the rest of my life, but I was also going to eat healthy, meditate, do yoga, and, basically come back looking like Sophia Vergara.

In the weeks leading up to me going, my mother was constantly calling me and giving me all these directions about what to do for "Princess". Of course, I was only half listening, because I had already decided that as soon as I got there I was going to ship that beast, I mean "pet," off to boarding school! So you can imagine my disappointment to find the kennel was closed for vacation. And I didn't know of another one.

In spite of that little setback, I really was able to relax. I did get my walks on the beach, well to the beach anyway, I might not have done yoga by the pool, but I did lounge by the pool, and even if I didn't exactly eat right, I did follow my doctor's orders and added salt to my diet by having a margarita for every meal.

I can tell you that spending some time alone at the beach was the absolute best thing I have done for myself in a long time. I highly recommend it. Everyone needs time to recharge, relax, and reflect. My mom has already booked her cruise for next year, and I told her I would love to keep her dog again, but what was the name of her kennel she was using now, just in case I had an emergency?

Oh, yeah, I even got some writing done- and I've got the post cards to prove it!

BLOWING SMOKE

Have you ever found yourself in a situation in which you were being judged by someone, but realized it only after the situation has passed? Oh, how many things come to your mind that you would have said if only you had realized while it was happening. This happened to me one time several years ago and it has stayed with me ever since.

I try my very best to be a good role model for my kids. I mean, we all do, right? And many times we draw upon our own experiences when we are sharing something with them or teaching them something. I have so many fond memories from my childhood growing up, and I have always enjoyed re-creating some of those same memories with my own children. So you can imagine my excitement when one day I walked into the quick stop with my kids, and saw that they had candy cigarettes for sale! I remember how much fun my brothers and cousins and I used to have buying those and I hadn't seen any since I was a kid. Trust me, the candy ones are much harder to find than the real ones. Anyway, I was so excited to show them all the different "brands" and I bought them several boxes. When we walked outside I couldn't wait to show them the little red "light" on the tip, how we used to hold them between our fingers, and how we would nibble them down to pretend we were smoking.

So there we were, standing outside the store by the dumpster, sharing a bonding experience, passing along a fun childhood memory of mine nibbling away on our candy cigarettes, when I heard a loud voice yelling. I looked up to see a woman that I had seen in the store, standing there with her two daughters. She was looking at us with a deep, disapproving scowl on her face and was talking in a very angry voice about how disgusting smoking was, and what a terrible thing it was for someone to do that to their children. At first we all turned and looked around thinking she was talking to someone else, but then realized she was talking to us! But I couldn't process it fast enough, and they stormed away and disappeared around the corner before I had a chance to say anything to defend us. My kids were looking at me with quizzical looks on their faces, expecting me to say something that would explain this intrusion into our good time. All I could say was that she must have been having a bad day. I was actually thinking that she must have really needed a cigarette, badly!

Now, I have never smoked, and I grew up eating and playing with candy cigarettes. I am not campaigning for them one-way or the other. I will leave that to politics. I'm just saying that I was minding my own business, having fun with my kids, not doing anything to bother anybody, nothing illegal, when someone saw to it to come pass judgment on us and actually go out of their way to come into our space and make their unsolicited opinion known, and loudly, I might add. Maybe it's just a natural by-product of the fact that we are all constantly being asked to weigh in on our opinions; text to vote for the next voice or dance talent, give the thumbs up or thumbs down on the article we read. Of course, we are all entitled to our opinions, but should we sit in judgment of everyone, all the time, and hand down the sentences loud and clear without being asked? Where do we draw the line at speaking our minds just because we don't like what we see? (Of course, I am talking about common sense here. Not life and death situation.) I don't always walk out the door armed with a well thought out defensive argument in mind for whatever candy I might decide to buy that day.

Unfortunately, I didn't think of anything to say at the time, probably for the best. It's not always wise to speak out in the heat of the moment. But I have always wanted to let that woman know that my kids are practically grown now, and they don't smoke either. Well.... not cigarettes. In fact, my kids didn't like the taste of the candy cigarettes, and after I had them that day, I remembered that I didn't really like the taste of them either. In fact, they said if the real cigarettes tasted anything like the candy ones, they didn't want anything to do with them. Maybe a real deterrent would be for all drugs to have a candy version that tastes like chalk. It's a shame they've practically banned them.

So, trying to be a responsible adult and steer kids from the dangers of smoking, I always give out candy cigarettes for Halloween. I just hope I can find them in the store hidden somewhere behind the real ones.

I SLEPT MY WAY TO THE TOP!

This year is one of the "Big Ones," a major high school reunion, and I must admit that I am a little nervous about going. It's not that I'm worried about how I look, or how much I've changed since we last saw each other. The reason is that it is so strange to find out the things that people remember about you. And it can be unnerving to hear their memories. Years ago, at our last reunion, I found out that my high heels had poked a hole in a boy's leather seat of his convertible-and I never knew that until he told me at the reunion. I'm afraid what people will tell me about me because, I admit that I had a reputation for sleeping around, and well deserved, too, I might add.

Just to clarify, I am an advocate for it, and I highly recommend it to anyone who is looking for a way to advance in their current situation, or in any area of life, really. The important thing to remember is that it's all in the timing, and once you get in the right position and the nice, steady rhythm of breathing going, well, in no time at all, you will think you're dreaming. I just really don't believe there is any easier way to get ahead than by giving yours a rest. The truth is that just a little short nap during the day helps boost your brain function and helps you stay focused on tasks. There is even research to back me up on this. I tried to explain all this way back in high school to my teachers who were frustrated that I kept nodding off in their class, like it was personal or something. You would have thought the health benefits of a nap were obvious, especially in Biology, of all subjects!

But, no! I was always put in charge of things like the remote to change the slides when the beeper beeped on the slide show. I am sure the intention was to keep me awake, and it might have worked (LOL!) if they hadn't, in fact, turned off the lights to project the slide show, which of course just made it that much more conducive for me to get a really good 30 minute nap and feel completely refreshed for the rest of my afternoon classes. This was a problem for me, because there were those students in class who were always irritated that we would get so far behind in the slides and actually accused me for their poor grades. It is these people that I am reluctant to see at the reunion. The thing is, that I would always wake up from my little school induced slumber knowing everything that they had discussed, like it had seeped its way into my subconscious mind. So I don't know what their problem was, I can only assume that they were awake, but daydreaming. Any teacher I had after I took my little nap thought I was a model student, showing up for class all energized and ready to learn.

This continued all through high school, and I can't tell you what wonders a little beauty rest will do for your teenage skin! I found that eventually, I just couldn't help giving in to a little siesta. In fact, I even started to take Spanish, thinking that I could actually get a grade for it-talk about an easy "A", but then, I heard that the French take off the whole afternoon (and the entire month of August, too!) so I took that instead. Although we didn't get to actually take a siesta, I did manage to catch a few winks in that class (thanks to that glowing skin!). And it didn't hurt my ability to learn French at all. I use it all the time; it comes in very handy when I am ordering Champagne and filet mignon.

My need for a little "nooner" has never changed. But the most challenging time for me to give in to it was when my children were pre-school age. Starting when they were about three years old, I spent the next seven years sleepwalking. Wouldn't you know that pre-school pick up time was at 12:30, right in the middle of my best REM? The worst though, was when they were late getting out and I had to wait. Nothing is quite as embarrassing as having the teachers wake you up by knocking on your car window because you are holding up the car pool traffic. Oh, you can pretend all you want that you were just reading, or filing your nails, but the drool running down your chin is a dead giveaway, as is your slurred speech, and the frightened, confused look in your eyes.

But the absolute worst time for me was when my daughter wanted to play Barbie (which thankfully was a short lived phase). Just the word "Barbie" had a hypnotic affect on me and immediately sent me into a mini-coma like state. This was not helped by the fact that she would not let me do anything that I wanted to do with Barbie. "No, Barbie isn't going to catch on fire cooking in the kitchen! She is going to sleep in her princess bed." I was just trying to keep it interesting, and maybe have Fireman Ken come save her, just so I could stay awake, but, basically, I was just watching my daughter play Barbie and it was pure torture. I tried everything to stay interested and involved, but I just ended up being startled awake by the sound of her pulling everything out of the refrigerator trying to pour her self something to drink. I was always tempted to offer her a little shot of Vodka (but why waste it on someone who won't appreciate it, right?) but settled on Benadryl instead, just to try and get a little desperately needed shut-eye.

I have always felt sorry for, and wanted to defend the mom that I have read about being arrested and charged with child negligence because they found her three-year-old child wandering down the railroad tracks alone. She was probably a good, sleep deprived Barbie playing mother who couldn't keep her eyes open any longer, and whose child was a "Houdini" at picking any lock in the house. And, by the way, I wondered, where is the dad? The articles never mention him. If so, it would probably say something like, "The father was not charged, as he was assuming the child was safely in the mother's care, while he was taking a nap in the bedroom before going to work for his night job." Well, #@*$ the mom has a night job, too! Oh, so sorry, I didn't mean to sound angry there, I must be tired.

As for that boy's leather seat that I found out I tore with my heels, it happened when I was riding in his convertible in the homecoming parade, no matter what you were thinking. I still can't decide if I am going to my high school reunion or not. I think I will go lie down and sleep on it.

RISKY BUSINESS

There I was, standing with the door open, trying to make a crucial decision, one that could possibly have severe consequences, life threatening, even, when I realized that pretty much everything in life is a risk. Literally, every single day we are faced with potential life and death situations, and eating something out of my mom's refrigerator was no exception. From the way I felt, all light-headed and dizzy, I had two options. With option number one, I could decide not to eat something from her fridge and chance perishing from starvation, but hold out hope that someone would come back just in time to force a bite of, hopefully, freshly made sandwich, preferably a grilled grouper one, into my mouth right before I took my last gasp of breath. Or, with option number two, I could take a chance, and make a sandwich using what appeared to be the last remaining piece of what looked and smelled to be turkey, or maybe ham, or corned beef, (or was it dog food?) and some mayonnaise. At least it was a mayonnaise jar, but without the label on it I couldn't be sure, especially given my mom's propensity for reusing containers (and even old, used aluminum foil, for that matter). Either way, it looked like a slow and painful death was all that awaited me-by starvation or food poisoning. Then again, I was thinking as I stood there, on the brink of near collapse, maybe the label just came off. Maybe that was a fresh jar of mayonnaise, or maybe it's not mayonnaise at all. Maybe I was putting way too much emphasis on the whole "use by date" on the label thing, as my mother suggests. According to my mom, nothing really ever goes bad, especially given the amount of preservatives they put in everything nowadays. My mom insists it's just a ploy by the food companies to get you to buy more of their product. These thoughts were going through my head as I stood there with the refrigerator door open. Maybe I was just hallucinating, teetering on the brink of famine. But I couldn't help thinking that even if it wasn't the food's expiration date it might just be my own.

Actually, one of the first things I try to do when I get to my mom's house is to try, very quietly, to go through the contents of her fridge and throw out everything that looks like it could be a death threat. I do not want to hurt her feelings, this is a very touchy subject. So I try to do it covertly, which is not easy, because her little dog, sweet, precious, little thing, comes running excitedly into the kitchen, barking, whenever she hears anyone in there. I can't decide if she is trying to warn me and stop me from accidental food poison, or letting my mom know what I am up to (the little bitch). I am tempted to give her a little bit of the things I pull from the fridge and see what happens, but figure that might actually be too risky. Instead, I decide to try it on her bird. It completely serves her right for waking me up with "Early bird gets the worm, early bird gets the worm" at the crack of dawn every morning. I decide that is too risky, too.

Everyday there are dozens of risky decisions for us to assess. I made a list of just a few that I found myself pondering recently, and thought I would share them here with you, as any good glamorous girlfriend would. And while they are not life and death, thank goodness, you might have found yourself evaluating some of the very same ones. If so, I hope you choose wisely, for the choice you make could have a profound effect on how fulfilling, exciting, or long your life will be.

For instance; should I go out the door after getting ready without taking a last look in my magnifying mirror? Now that my eyesight is not as sharp as it once was, this could be a potentially embarrassing situation. I have seen people that have taken this risk, and the odds were not in their favor that day. But sometimes you just have to run out, because time has. Sometimes I risk it. You will know if you see me, so just smile, and don't say anything.

Should I sing out as loud as possible to my favorite song when I am in my car? Even if the windows are down and I am at a stoplight? Even if I don't know all of the words in that one little section? Even if my cat does come and bite me on the knee whenever I sing out loud? I say YES! Because-it is my favorite song!! Not life and death.

Dare I wear a swimsuit at Spring Break? Before Easter? Hmmmm… absolutely not, I thought white was out before Easter. Way too risky for you, dear readers. I am just thinking of you.

Dare I turn on the television at night and chance seeing a Kardashian and ruining a perfectly good night's sleep? Much too risky!

Like I said, there are many choices to make every day, some more riskier than others. Some are life and death decisions. Most are not, thankfully. Most of the time there is a compromise. Most of the time you take calculated risks, not foolish behaviors that could get you in real trouble.

I decided, after careful inspection of the contents of my mom's refrigerator, not to chance the mayo or the mystery meat. I know that being too risk obverse, constantly asking "What if," can paralyze you with fear, and I know too, about all the wonders that a little paralyzing from botulism can do for you. However, I am not convinced my mom has a license to grow it in a home laboratory. I did find a jar of mustard that was just 10 months past the "use by date" and a dusty, only slightly rusted can of tuna in the back of her pantry, and even though there was no bread, I found a box of only slightly stale crackers, barely a year past the "Best by" date, so I took my chances and ate that. And it's a good thing, too, because I would have surely expired from hunger since no one came back with the car for several more hours. It is a good thing that I am an adventurous type. If your mom is anything like my mom, you must enjoy living on the edge when you go home to visit.

Maybe I am being a little too cautious. My kids have accused me of letting things linger too long in our own refrigerator. But they are taking things too far. Bottled salad dressing really never does go bad, so I don't understand why they refuse to eat it. 2007 was not so very long ago, either, I remember it well. It was a very good year, and for salad dressing, too, I'm sure.

P.S. My mother wasn't amused by this column and felt the need to defend herself, so she sent this rebuttal:

From: Mary C.

"My daughter recently published an article about "Mom's Refrigerator." Before I sue her for slander, I would like to state my case: This was from someone who thinks pickles expire at midnight on the date "use before" or "good by" on the bottle! People smoke cigarettes with the WARNING! THIS MAY CAUSE CANCER! But oh, no - don't eat pickles after midnight on the day of the "use by" date! And you can take that article with a grain of salt. By the way salt lasts for decades! Have you ever thrown out salt? And what about spices? Don't they last forever??? What about the C-rations that the troops used in WWII? Did they have expiration dates? I can just imagine a soldier in the middle of nowhere saying, "Gee, this has expired! Throw it away." Growing up, I remember my grandmother and other relatives canning food and keeping them for years in a cellar. As far as I know, no one died from eating them. My thought is if the can isn't pouched out, then it's good. My great aunt and uncle lived in the country without electricity and kept their milk and eggs in a well house where well water ran through a trough keeping them from going bad. They also had a "smoke house" - no, not that kind of smoke house - they hung meat in it and cured it. Sometimes it had a little "green" on it, but they just cut it off. Nothing wrong with that, I say. I ate lots of the hams done this way. I didn't die or even get sick. In fact, it was the best ham ever! (They lived into their 90s - e-coli? never heard of back then). I mean, what is a little "fuzz" on strawberries - just cut it off. By the way, I just "found" a package of Jell-O in my pantry with no "date" on it - does that mean it is good forever? I'm keeping it! Well, I must admit that this morning I did clean out my fridge (unaware at the time about the article) and I did come across a can or two of Crisco shortening with expiration dates of 2007 - but, hey, it still looked good to me - but, reluctantly I threw it out, just to make my daughter happy!"

Thanks, Mom!:) I feel a little safer now, but I am wondering how I managed to survive my childhood.

PAYING FOR MY PLEASURE

Paying for pleasure is one of the oldest transactions in history, and yet some people still seem to find it an unsavory idea. I really don't see anything wrong with it myself. In fact, I think it's a rather nice arrangement. I think you should expect a fair and reasonable experience when you pay a basic price, and then, if you want something a little more, you should have the option to pay for it. I was recently given the opportunity of paying for an extra two inches, and I immediately jumped on it! It might be a guilty pleasure, enjoying an extension like that, but if you have done any flying recently, you probably agree with me, and would have done the same. What do they expect you to do with your legs on those long flights, especially in 6" heels? In a case like that, I am willing to pay an almost obscene amount of money for just two more inches if that would make it a much more pleasurable experience. So, I upgraded to first class. It's just good, old capitalism at work. Sadly, it all seems to have gotten a bad reputation over the years.

The more I started thinking about it, the more I realized that there are many other situations in which I would gladly hand over a few extra dollars in order to get a more satisfying experience. I don't mind tipping people for the extra effort they give. In fact, I think it's a great incentive. I willingly pay a bit more when someone goes the extra mile, or inches, for me. Sometimes that extra push makes all the difference in the experience. But, now, people want you to tip them for doing nothing more than the basics. I am expected to pay extra for an experience in which the other person contributed nothing extra for me. Sounds like a bad relationship to me. Call me old fashioned, but you shouldn't expect me to pay you for taking care of myself.

It seems the whole concept of taking care of the customer has come to an end. It's difficult to get any customer service at all these days, let alone paying for an upgrade. This is a disturbing trend. I am especially leery of those restaurants that want me to clean my own dishes- not just throw away some paper and plastic, but actually clean the dishes, and sort them into collection bins! Where is the outrage? I don't like doing that. Why do you think I am out eating and not at home? I don't want to have to clean up after my self. That's what I am paying you to do.

Which brings me to my most disappointing loss, the disappearance of full service "Service Stations." I was more than happy to pay for someone to service me-I mean, my car. Now, self-serve is the way everybody is going. Don't get me wrong, I am not against being self-serving, all I am saying is that I would like to have the option whether to look under my own hood, or have someone else do it to me, I mean FOR me. And, personally, I don't like that *I* am expected to do the pumping! I always thought that was the man's job. I guess there are some women who enjoy that part of it, but again, I would just like for there to be options for us that want to pay somebody else for these types of personal services. This is a service economy after all, and I, for one, think it's great to be able to pay to be serviced.

And I thought about the grocery store, too. They use to employ all those cute bag boys, and getting bagged was once part of the normal service, then it changed to where you could tip the guys to bag your groceries for you, and now it's all on you to take care of yourself. It's gone to self-checkout and there's not even the option, not one cute boy to be found that you could offer a little extra money to, to help take care of a most basic need. It's just not as much fun anymore. I don't know about you, but I find that most of the time doing it by your self is overrated. I say bring back the boys to bag me, I am willing to pay for them. Okay, okay, bring the girls, too. Have it your way.

And that's all I want, is to have my way- I'll gladly pay for it.

TONE DEAF

Reading can be so informative. Just recently I read an article that said parents were no longer enrolling their children in piano lessons and predicted that the instrument was on its way to becoming extinct, except perhaps in Japan, which must be why our piano is a Yamaha. It was such a dire prediction for piano teachers, and I'm guessing for piano makers, piano tuners, and piano music composers, as well. I feel so sad for Schroeder. No one, but for Lucy, will understand what he is doing in just a few short years. However, the people I feel most concerned for are parents.

September is usually filled with not only the sounds of moans and groans about homework, and early bed times, and ringing alarm clocks, but also the whining and pleading and screams from the kids about piano lessons. It is a time-honored tradition and I fear for its demise. The article stated that children's attention spans were no longer equipped to handle the time and focus and attention it takes to master scales. I can't believe parents believe this. All you have to do is see just how many times a child can repeatedly ask you the same question, such as, "why not?" when you tell them that they can not do something. They can keep it up without pause for hours on end, days if necessary, if it is something they really want, like to go on a three day motorcycle trip with their friend Johnny-who just got his motorcycle license, and motorcycle, yesterday, and is already fourteen-duh! Kids do, in fact, have laser-like focus that knows no time limits if it's something that they want. And, believe me, they have that same attention and focus if it's something that they don't want. Parents must be able to hold their own.

The problem is, parents have it all wrong. Piano lessons are not for the child. Learning to play the piano is not about teaching the child the beauty of music, or instilling in them the merits of self-discipline, or even something they will be able to put on their resume in six more years. In fact, piano lessons are not about the kids at all. They are about the parents. Kids just think everything is always about them.

Would any sane parent really put themselves through the torture of repeatedly listening to the same six notes being plunked out, over and over like Chinese Water Torture? Would they bring it upon themselves to listen to the same missed notes that sound like a dying cat that make you grind your teeth to stumps, and dig your nails deep into your flesh, every day, for weeks at a time, just for the betterment of their kids? Of course not! Would we seriously commit to thousands of dollars in music lessons and the actual purchase of a piano, not to mention the hours of time spent driving and waiting at music lessons just so our children can angrily pound out "Jingle Bells" during the family Christmas carol sing-a-long? Do we put ourselves through the anxiety of actually having to come face to face with "The Piano Teacher" when she asks us if we helped little Billy with his lessons by setting up a practice time and encouraging him, and risking her wrath if we offer our apologies and excuses for why it didn't work out this week? No! We do it for one reason and one reason only-to become tone deaf.

What the parents today are failing to realize is that if you have not put yourself through the pains of piano lessons, and the flailing and protests, and tears and crying, and head-banging numbness that go with them, how will you ever learn to tune out your children when they become teenagers? I tell you, you won't stand a chance standing up to their angry outbursts and accusations of your trying to ruin their lives when they are fifteen, if you haven't learned to let them fall on deaf ears when they are seven. Piano practice is for you, the parent to practice the technique of the "Parental Tune Out." Getting through the excruciating pain of wrong keys is critical, but the most important practice is not giving in to their cries and pleading not to have to practice, or go to class, or even have to take piano lessons in the first place. These are the real sounds you must learn to mute. In time you will be amazed at how easily you are able to have absolutely no desire to throw something, or to put a plastic bag over your head, not only during the actual "music" practice, but also, how that translates into not wanting to scream back or gag them with the towel, when they are screaming at you and slamming the door to their bedroom because you asked them to please pick up their wet towel they left laying in the bathroom floor. Music lessons will save you and your family. They are the key to holding it all together.

When you are tone deaf you will no longer hear that mocking, grating tone that teenagers have a way of inserting into the most mundane and briefest statement, the sound that insinuates that they do not think you have a clue about anything. This is a critical skill to master and must be accomplished through the constant practice along with your child learning the proper finger positions and all the major scales. These are not minor concerns, I assure you, and if you don't want them to become major, practice with due diligence. You will be glad you did when the big day comes of the "Piano Recital." The weeks leading up to it are some of the most important training you will receive. When you find that you can actually stay awake and keep your head up and your eyes open, clap when appropriate, nod and smile, and not have the faintest idea that it has been two hours and your child still hasn't played, you deserve a happy face. And once your child does play, and you don't hear that he or she missed the note that they have been practicing not to miss for the whole year, and you don't hear the bitter resentment in their voice when you tell them "Good job!" then you know you are deserving of a gold star. You have officially become tone deaf!

On another positive note, being tone deaf is not just for use on the kids, it works just as well on adults. For instance, after you have been together for, say, twenty five years or more (this is a personal disclaimer and is in no way related to me or any one I know personally) the thing that saves countless relationships is the ability to completely tune out the other person. And I firmly believe this can only be accomplished from getting through years of your children's piano lessons.

So go, I implore you! Enroll your children in those piano lessons now, before it's too late! In doing so, you are doing yourself a favor. Trust me. I hope I have helped save your sanity, your family, your marriage, and maybe the piano business, too. That would be music to my ears.

FACING FEARS AND FAUXBIAS: OLD AGE, NEW AGE, ANTI-AGE

I used to love getting scared when I was a kid. When we went to the fair I loved riding all of the roller coasters that went fast and turned you upside down, and the double Ferris wheel that took you really high up in the air. When I was a teenager I used to love watching all the scary movies that came on television, and I especially liked going to the haunted houses at Halloween. Even though you were scared half to death, it was fun and you knew you were safe, and probably even knew some of the "monsters." In fact, more often than not, they were my classmates at school. Recently however, I found myself in another scary house, with a friend of mine, and let me tell you, it was a real House of Horrors! I didn't realize at the time quite what I had gotten myself into when I told her that I would go with her, and when she said she was going to face her fears, she meant literally!

We had noticed an ad for a skin spa that implored you to come to them when you noticed "The First Signs of Aging." I am pretty sure that happens in infancy when you begin turning over, sitting up, and achieving all of those developmental milestones. Nonetheless, we decided to check it out and made reservations, and I immediately started having some myself when I stepped through the door.

Upon arriving, we found ourselves standing inside a cold, white, sterile room that appeared to be a laboratory of some kind, and right away, I was blinded by a glaringly bright, white light of the most dreaded kind: a fluorescent light! After my eyes adjusted and I was able to see again I saw the scariest sight of all; the room was completely surrounded by mirrors, fluorescent lights and mirrors! I was left to face my biggest fear: myself! And under such harsh and cruel conditions, too. A few minutes later I was approached by two horrible looking monsters wearing scary masks of mud and clay, and one of them looked like

The Creature from the Black Lagoon all covered in seaweed. Then a "Dr." came in wearing a lab coat and carrying a magnifying mirror, and as he began talking to me, a horror movie began playing on a large screen behind him showing some of the "procedures" they were proposing to perform on me. They could inject me with poison to paralyze my muscles, or burn my upper level of skin off with acid. He explained how he was going to stretch, and cut, and vacuum suck me from the inside, and that I could get stapled, and lasered, and peeled, and then all sewn up again. I saw myself looking just like a regular *Frankenstein's Monster.* He started discussing how all of this was going to be good for my mental state, too. I said I thought he was approaching some fine lines, here, and he said he could erase those, too, that these procedures were not just for deep-set problems.

My head was reeling. I began to sweat and feel nauseous. My head was throbbing and my knees were week. I started to have a panic attack. I mean, was this the only option? How could I get out, besides death being the only answer? How was I ever going to stop the hands of time clawing across my entire body without resorting to the torture chambers? Was there no antidote that I could just ingest? Couldn't I just drink some pleasant fruity tasting anti-aging serum that works from the outside in, something with no book of dangerous side effects? But wait, it began to dawn on me, like the harsh morning light, that I've already been drinking the Kool-Aid. And, it does have harmful side effects; it's causing me to consider voluntarily checking myself into this chamber of horrors, and to pay good money for it, too.

It seems that aging is the only thing we are truly afraid of. It's a paradox, really: time is the one thing we all want more of, but we don't want to have to face it. That's why there are products and services being shoved at us morning, noon, and night preying upon this fear, offering us a chance to turn back the clock and stop time in it's tracks, or, at least the visible signs of time. I just wish I noticed it happening to me sooner. Then I could have stopped the tracks of time before they had started marching across my face. I even began to regret that I didn't call the doctor for my kids and immediately have them injected with youth serum to keep them babies. I actually came to regret it even more, later, when they became teenagers. I guess I have been absorbed in other things, like living my life, enjoying the outdoors, sharing lots of laughs, and anguishing over what to cook for dinner every night for the last twenty years. Clearly these things did not serve me well. I should not have been giving in to my feelings and making actual facial expressions. I just didn't know any other way to convey that I was having fun, or tired, or about to go crazy. And now I am facing the consequences, literally. And I am scared.

But I try not to pass along my fears to my children, especially my daughter; I don't want her to start worrying about expressing herself yet, she's only eighteen. However, I think it might be too late. When I was touring college campuses with her, I noticed at the campus bookstores they were selling anti-aging products, all targeted to the 18-22 year old female demographic. I mean, really, how dare they start showing any signs of maturity? I complimented one young woman we saw shopping there on her youthful appearance, and asked her which products she used and she said her mom had started injecting her with anti-aging products *in utero*. I am surprised she reached full term. The interesting thing seems to be that as we continue to look younger than our actual age, we continue to act younger than our age, too.

It seems adolescence is lasting twenty years longer. Now *that* is really frightening!

It turns out that we really do know all of the monsters that haunt us, the ones hiding under our beds, in our closets, and in our minds, because we create them. These aren't real fears, they are just faux-bias, fed to us by the media, and it's up to us to decide what we let get under our skin. We can let our worst fears come to light and try and trick ourselves with Dr. Plastic, but I think I will just continue to try getting along on hair color, teeth whitening, hair removal creams, makeup, fake tans, push-up bras, dressing all in black, candles, and denial for as long as possible. There is comfort in staying in the dark. I will become like a vampire, only venturing out after dark. After all, they are seeking immortality, too. Or, maybe I will find immortality by contributing something positive to the world and leaving it behind after I've gone.

I don't know though, the pressure to fight the aging process is intense. I've recently noticed some of those spots showing up on my hands; thank goodness animal prints are still in. And, I recently noticed those menacing little age lines beginning to creep in around my mouth. I guess I shouldn't have shaved my moustache. In an effort to get this all under control without resorting to the torture chambers just yet, I decided to try some of the newest anti-aging products now on the market. I spent about two hours at the skin care counter trying to read the tiny print on the smallest jars of creams I have ever seen. Surely, if this stuff worked I would need more than was in those tiny jars. My eyes became blurry. Apparently, blurry eyes make you look so much better, because I found a product called Miracle Blur. I was certain that it would produce the same affect as rubbing Vaseline in your eyes, or in the eyes of those around you. It was probably just a fancier and more expensive version. Imagine my surprise, then, after I bought some and took it home and used it when, low and behold, it worked, just as they promised! I did once again have the skin of a teenager; I broke out all over my face. I began to think that aging just might not be the scariest part of all this after all.

And then I saw an advertisement suggesting that you give someone you love and care about the gift of plastic surgery. It seemed like the perfect, and least invasive, solution to this whole anti-aging problem. So, now, I am not worried at all that I am going to end up looking just like my mother. Because, for her last birthday, I gave my mom plastic surgery, and now I am going to end up looking just like Sophia Vergara!

LEFT IS RIGHT, TOO

I love our Christmas tree. Whether we have chosen it ourselves from the Boy Scout's parking lot, or had the great fortune to have some dear friends bring us one back from their Christmas tree farm in North Carolina, we always have the perfect Christmas tree. When we first get it we always let it stand a few days to fully open up before we decorate it. Filling the house with its wonderful pine fragrance, the tree makes the house smell like the holiday season. Every year we declare that particular tree to be the prettiest one that we have ever had. Every year it's the perfect size, just the right height, and the prettiest shape. No matter how many limbs we have to trim off, or how many inches we have to saw off the bottom, it ends up being the perfect size, it really does. Even if we have sawed off too many inches because of the crooked trunk that we didn't see at first, it is still exactly the right height after we set it on the ice chest. And after we wrap a white sheet of "snow" around the base, no one could ever tell that 6 ft. tree is now only 2 ½ feet tall. And, after we get it in place and stand back to admire it, I just know it will fit the space beautifully, if we could just turn it a little to the right, because it is leaning ever so slightly to the left. Not much, but just enough to be obviously off balance. Now, it's almost there, but just a little over rotated, so back to the left a bit, a bit more, almost there. By this time, I can tell that I better get my Darling Husband a drink. Because, I hate to tell him, I really do, but it is still leaning way too far right for me. This is our Christmas tree and it must be as straight and stable as possible to hold all the beautiful trimmings that we are going to place on it and underneath it. And, being centered brings the most stability and balance… doesn't it?

After we have both had a drink, or two, we decide that we should probably secure the tree to the wall, because we don't want it to fall over when I go to water it, like the one did a couple of years ago. It is way too traumatic and stressful, being home alone, caught under a Christmas tree, covered with broken glass from favorite ornaments and lights that have been shattered, and with all the presents that were so carefully wrapped in beautiful Christmas papers now soggy with water. It's even more traumatic than your kids catching you lying under the tree with Santa, trust me. All you can really do at that point is pull yourself out as carefully as possible, soak up as much of the water and roll up the carpet as best you can, close the door to the room, post a sign that says "Santa Says Have a Drink Before You Enter," have a well stocked bar, and drink for the rest of the day.

So, after getting the tools and wiring the tree into the corner, we both agree that it is now as straight as it is going to be, so we decide to only look at the tree from the left corner of the room. From that angle it looks perfect. And it is from that spot that we invite our family and guests to come over and gaze at the tree when they are here during the holidays.

When the tree is securely in place, it is time for our favorite part, decorating it. I love this. Now, we do not have a "designer tree." While they are lovely, my favorite kind of tree is a "homemade" tree, filled with ornaments and memories made and collected over the years. The only two things that are new on our tree each year are the paper chain, which we make out of red, green, blue, and yellow construction paper every year (although some years we have only been able to find packs of construction paper with purple and pink, instead of true red and blue, but, we decided that next to the twinkling colored lights, you really wouldn't be able to tell. Especially if you just looked at the tree from the far left corner of the room.). The other new decoration we put on the tree each year are the candy canes. I love having candy on the tree, and the kids have always loved hanging them, it was one of their favorite things to help with when they were too little to handle the fragile glass ornaments that we used to have. As we are decorating the tree and Christmas music is playing softly in the background, and the colored lights are twinkling, I enjoy standing back and watching the scene, admiring how beautiful our tree is this year, when I suddenly see that someone is putting on the candy canes all wrong. All the candy canes on the bottom half of the tree are on backwards, all hanging to the left! "Who, in the Hell..." I asked, "is putting the candy canes on backwards?"

(Maybe I'd had one drink too many) And then I saw my sweet little left-handed angel happily hanging candy canes, lost in the joy of the moment, admiring her work. And with a little tear in my eye, I said a little silent prayer of thanks that she didn't hear me, and I stood back right where I was and saw the prettiest Christmas tree we have ever had. I realized that whether I look at it from the far left, slightly to the right, upside down (some people hang them from the ceiling-no lie), backwards, or somewhere in the middle, it is our Christmas tree. Just like us, it is not perfect, no matter how much we like to try and control things, and we don't all see the same things the same way but those differences are all of our personalities blended into it, and that makes it very much our family Christmas tree. And this year's tree is our prettiest one, ever.

I wish everyone the Merriest Christmas and Happiest Holidays, ever, no matter how you look at it!

LET'S TALK TOFURKEY
(WARNING: THIS ARTICLE IS NOT POLITICALLY CORRECT AND MAY CONTAIN OFFENSIVE MATERIAL)

I've been busy planning the Thanksgiving menu and searching for and organizing all of my recipes. Now I'm starving. These are some of my favorite foods that I look forward to having all year because we only have them for the Thanksgiving lunch. Then, with the click of the mouse, the excitement was all taken away when I was Skyping with my daughter, and she reminded me of her recent dietary lifestyle changes. Just how far does one go for the sake of family harmony, especially, at the holidays?

When Daughter Dear came home from college for Spring Break last year, she informed us that she had become a vegetarian. Which, really, I figured that was her problem, not ours. Surely, she could be around our fried chicken and burgers for a week. I mean, I try and be supportive, but for someone who grew up on, and still enjoys a nice juicy steak, I just don't see why we *all* had to be vegetarian. But then, when she came home for the summer she informed us that she was now vegan. I wondered if salmon was going to count. I figured I should at least learn the difference between vegetarian and vegan. And, then it became our problem. Three months was going to be a long time without pizza.

It turns out that being vegan means not just giving up meat, but to also give up all animal by-products, such as cheese, which was like asking me to give up my leather boots. Next thing I know I will be asked to give up my furs. Your loyalties can be tested. Does it never end? It was a long three months of faking it. Have you ever tasted tofurkey?

At the end of the summer, after we dropped off Darling Daughter at the airport for her to head back to school, we immediately drove to Ruth's Chris and ordered a filet, bread with real butter, and topped it all off with a piece of chocolate cake for dessert, real chocolate cake-not some fake tofu hybrid. By this time, I even wanted a real cigarette, and I don't smoke.

My fear this holiday season is that she will come home for Thanksgiving announcing that she is now a fruitarian-and will only eat fruit, or, even worse, that she has become a "breatharian," and will only live on air. I started to panic, I can't breathe just thinking about it.

I could just see us now, all sitting around the dining table for the Thanksgiving meal connected to our oxygen tanks. I wonder if oxygen comes in roast turkey flavor? I remember actually seeing oxygen bars when we were in Las Vegas a few months ago. In fact, everyone in Las Vegas is hooked on oxygen. Maybe being a breatharian was the new black. Then it occurred to me that instead of flying the kids all the way home for Thanksgiving, my husband and I could just fly out there and we all meet halfway in Las Vegas. I feel certain Las Vegas would be the one place to have a Thanksgiving oxygen buffet.

But, no! I wanted everyone home to celebrate Thanksgiving. Then, I began to worry about how I would seat everyone at the Thanksgiving table. What about those that refused to live on oxygen? I didn't want to offend anyone. Would we have to have separate tables for the vegans and the vegetarians, in addition to the kid's table? And what about the people who will only eat organic food that is grown locally? Surely my apple pie made with apples flown in from Washington State, and real butter, isn't any more offensive to them than the smell of their organic, local grown kale is to me? What about separating the Democrats and the Republicans? Should I just put all the difficult people at the Auburn table? Can't we all just get along? Isn't food supposed to bring people together? In the historical narrative of breaking bread together I'm not sure anyone was asking if it was gluten free.

I finally decided to hell with it. Come Thanksgiving Day I will be enjoying my traditional meal of a real turkey with all the trimmings and my favorite cakes and pies and I don't care if my food traveled farther to get to my table than my kids did, I just want everyone together, thankful to be sitting at the same table. The vegans, vegetarians, carnivores, slow-food, farm-to-table, gourmet foodies, breatharians, and anything else I have never heard of, all enjoying our many blessings and the fact that we are fortunate enough to be that choosy. And I hope you are enjoying the same.

SKELETONS IN THE CLOSET

I am coming out of the closet. I just finished trying on everything in there and it's confirmed: I have nothing to wear. Absolutely. Nothing. To wear. How much time over the years have I spent searching around in there trying to find something to wear? Too much time, that's how much, and enough is enough! It's time to come right out and address the issue and to finally deal with any skeletons rattling around in there: all of those empty hangers that have shed their once beautiful clothing that is now lying in a heap somewhere on the floor, ghosts of shopping trips past; shirts, and sweaters, and slacks and dresses that once fit but are now shapeless, baggy, unspeakable horrors that are still hanging around in there collecting cobwebs, some with their price tags still dangling from their limp silhouettes. I will practically have to don a puffy jacket with some major shoulder pads to force my way into the back of my closet, and to protect me from the scratchy, itchy, scary, ugly things that should never again see the light of day. I'm sure I probably have one in there somewhere, with all of the other bad outfits from the eighties. I have always heard that what goes around, comes around, so I haven't gotten rid of those clothes yet. I feel it is just a matter of time before they will be back in style. However, my daughter has assured me, that that time will never come. I think she's right. I guess it's time to exercise (oops!), I mean exorcise, some of those past mistakes still haunting my closet and partake in that ancient, cleansing ritual known as Spring Cleaning.

After having spent the entire winter months wearing the same pair of black yoga pants, black pullover sweater, and fuzzy slippers, I greet the brightness of spring with a desire for a fresh start, for the chance to lighten up, in every way; my weight, my hair color, and my wardrobe. Every spring I gather up my courage and dare to venture back into the deep, dark recesses of my closet in search of some article of clothing hibernating in there that will aid in my rebirth and allow me to emerge as a younger, thinner, blonder and better-dressed version of myself, like a butterfly emerging from it's cocoon. Maybe the changing of the seasons makes me want to change myself. Whatever the reason may be, after the cold days of winter have passed, and it is time to dress for warmer weather, I walk into my closet and don't see myself anywhere in there. All I see are the bulky, dark winter clothes of the "old" me. What happened to all of my favorite thin clothes? It is apparent that I have nothing to wear. Or, maybe I just can't find anything with all of those clothes crammed in there.

All of the fashion magazines' spring editions are promising me that with a well-organized closet I would finally have an answer to one of life's most pressing questions: "What should I wear today?" I wonder if maybe, if I was just organized, I could find the "me" I am looking for in my closet, and not have to buy an entire new wardrobe. Maybe, among the once worn items that have become only a memory caught on Instagram, and the things that I tell myself that I might wear again one day when I lose that few pounds, or the items I intend to have mended, or the bags of clothes I'm going to exchange when I find the receipt, I might actually find myself again. I have read that you just have to look at your things with a different set of eyes, so I put on my glasses and headed into the abyss with my goal of decluttering my closet and coming out with *at least* two new outfits for the new me--things that I have never before worn together. To do this, I get completely dressed, including hair and makeup, put on my one favorite outfit, the only one that I can find that makes me feel really good about myself, and a pair of my favorite shoes, and step into my closet to do a little shopping. I just know that somewhere in there, among those clothes all crammed together, is a new outfit or two that is perfectly fitting for my new identity.

Now, I have considered hiring a fashion consultant to come in and help me with a wardrobe makeover and closet organization, but I would have to replace everything in there before I could let them see it, in the same way you always have to completely clean the house before the housekeepers show up. And, if I did hire a consultant I would have to make them sign an officially notarized document stating that they would never, ever breathe a word to anybody about what they saw. And then, unfortunately, I would still have to kill them. I just can't chance the glamorous people at The Amandas organizing team finding out about how unorganized my closet is.

The truth is that I like that my closet is full. I like walking into my closet and seeing it overflowing with clothes. So what if I only actually wear the same five things in there, or that most of the time I can't find what I am looking for, or that most of the clothes in there I outgrew long ago and have been in there so long that they are gathering dust? Who cares if the pile of clothes that I intend to have mended or altered or cleaned is bigger than the pile I actually wear? It *feels* like I have more clothes to wear. And that's what's important, how my clothes make me feel. I don't actually have to be wearing them to feel good. An overflowing closet gives me hope that somewhere among all of the various versions of me, the new me is in there, I just have to keep trying me on for size until I find myself. I'm afraid that if I take out all of my clothes that are stuffed in there, and only put back the ones that I have actually worn in the past year, that my closet will be a sad closet. A sad and empty tomb echoing with the hollow sound of only four pairs of pants and a handful of shirts, and no sign of life, of my life.

So, after spending all day on a flashback adventure of my entire adult life, pulling out every article of clothing I have ever bought in the last twenty years, frantically searching for something that I recognize as the "me" that I am now, I see it. It's the perfect accessory: a scarf that I found way in the back on the floor. I once read that a scarf can transform an LBD into 101 different outfits, and I have just pulled at least twenty-five Little Black Dresses out of my closet! Think how many new outfits that will be! Surely one of those would be the new "Me". I feel so much better. Now I can stop and put everything back and do spring cleaning next year.

MOTHER, MAY I?

Call me old fashioned, but in this day and age of virtual online games with people you don't really know, I still prefer playing the family games I grew up with; board games: card games, backyard games, I like them all. There is one childhood game in particular that I loved and it was "Mother, May I?" where you had to ask the caller or, "Mother," permission before you could do the task that you were told to perform. If you failed to ask "Mother, May I?" you had to go back. I played this all the time with my brothers and cousins and neighbors, and later on with my kids when they were little. I naively hoped it might convince them to ask my permission before they ever did anything questionable. LOL. However, I guess the game chips don't fall far from the kitchen table because my kids enjoy playing games, too, especially, with me. As it turns out, they have gotten particularly brilliant at playing mind games. And every Mother's Day they really tried to outdo them selves.

Each Mother's Day, my kids would conspiratorially tell me that they would let me sleep in on Mother's Day morning. It was a mandate, really. I knew, of course, that they wanted to bring me breakfast in bed, and I willingly played along with the game. It was while lying awake in bed one Mother's Day morning that it became all too clear to me, the lengths with which they would go to play mind games on me.

I would be awakened on Mother's Day morning by the crashing sounds of pots and pans banging around in the kitchen, and for the next hour I would pretend to be asleep. Finally, I would hear them whispering and giggling, and expected them to come "surprise" me at any minute. But, after the next hour, still lying there wide-awake, delirious from the smell of bacon and coffee and cinnamon rolls, it began to dawn on me their real intention, and it was not, I fear, just to let me know they were thinking of me by letting me sleep in.

I called my mom to tell her "Happy Mother's Day" and to let her know that I knew what the kids were planning for me for Mother's Day; they were planning to starve me to death. Either that, or they were not, in fact, thinking of me at all and had completely forgotten about me. After I hung up, feeling faint and weak in the knees, I made a lot of noise getting up to go to the bathroom and finally they came bouncing in with a cold breakfast of coffee, hard eggs and dry toast. They had eaten all of the cinnamon rolls "waiting on me to wake up."

But, this particular Mother's Day I had a better idea. I figured that there should be some sort of pay off for all that waiting, besides cold toast and KP duty. I know that motherhood is all about serving time for hard labor but I figured that for the time already served, I should be served my favorite cocktail on all the Mother's Days to come. Since they were going to be hanging around all year long the kids might as well go ahead and learn how to make my favorite drink, especially since they are the reason I do. And, too, I was certain that all that measuring would make learning math so much more fun. Besides, you know that I think it is a mother's duty to make sure her children do not step out into the world without a skill. Or they might come back. It seems that just when you finally start to get it all figured out, they pack up and leave for college, vowing never to move back home. They always do get your hopes up, don't they? And, they take their bartending skills with them to use for themselves.

On every Mother's Day since, my mom calls me and reminds me to put a granola bar in my bedside table. Except, I am sad to say, that this Mother's Day is the first one that I will not have either of my kids at home, since they are away at college. To make matters worse, I will be leaving a few days later to attend my son's college graduation. These are the trickiest mind games they have played on me yet. This just cannot be true. They did not ask me "Mother, May I grow up so fast?" I simply would not have allowed it. I would have said they had to go back to those long summer days of us playing in the sandbox, or picnicking in the park. I would not have given them permission to leave me alone on Mother's Day. Before they asked if they could take those steps into adulthood I would have said, "No, you may not." Motherhood is a lifetime sentence and one I am honored to serve. Now who is going to serve me my drink while rolling their eyes? I really do need one now.

Time plays the biggest mind games of all. I would like to have it all back. Mother Nature, may I?

~Cheers to my mom, my children, my mother-in-law, and all the moms out there!

P.S. I want to thank my darling daughter for giving me permission to use her photo. If you want to see how she really feels visit my website www.itsreallysunny.com

IT'S ABOUT BLOODY TIME

I'm envious of those of you who have patience. It must feel wonderful to feel as though time stands still for you. You are probably never worrying or hurrying because everything is working out just the way you planned it, all you need to do is to be patient. Well, good for you. I, unfortunately, am not blessed with it. And, boy, do I need it. So, I have decided that my New Year's Resolution this year is going to be to practice having more patience.

It seems to be a fact of life that patience is needed in almost every life situation, even in the most mundane and basic routine events, like waiting our turn for the bathroom first thing in the morning, or waiting on everyone to go out the door to work and school (oh, wait, someone's not going today? Someone's home sick, or working from home today? Extra patience is required.). In fact, even raising kids takes loads of patience; after all, eighteen years is a long time to wait! But, nothing compares to the patience that is required when going to get a manicure. Nothing even comes close. Not running errands and having to wait on the person in the car in front of me to finish texting so they can see that the light is green; not waiting on the red light to turn green, that I got stopped at when the person in front of me finished texting and looked up just in time to floor it through the yellow light and left me stopped at the red light. Not as much patience is required before I go in to order my lunch, because the people that are going to take my order, and make my lunch, do not really care whether I am ready to order or not. It's true that I must patiently wait and be ready when they are. I dare not burden them or irritate them any more than I already have by deciding to go there and do business with them and hand over my money to them. But again, I tell you, no other situation in life compares to the patience that is required when going to get a manicure. It requires multi-level patience.

Just think about it; first thing when you walk in, they assure you that they have time to do a manicure and ask you to go ahead and choose your color. This, by the way, is the first test for your patience, because I don't know about you, but I can't quite make up my mind between "Bubble Bath" and "Champagne Cocktail," or any of the fourteen other slightly various shades of pale, but I feel it is a critical decision, or there wouldn't be so many choices, so I must take my time and choose wisely. In truth, I can't really tell them apart at all, but their names are so intriguing I am convinced that the one I choose will have a profound effect on how my life will be when I leave the salon. I mean "Italian Love Affair" has the promise of so many life altering possibilities, but what if I choose "You're a Pisa Work," instead? Does that mean I will be leaning slightly to the left when I leave the salon? Not that I don't already. Anyway, having finally passed this test and chosen the same color that I choose every time I get a manicure, I am now told that they will be with me in a minute. So I sit down and pick up the latest issue of *People* magazine, and this is the second test of my patience, because after flipping through twenty-two pages of the latest news on Kim Kardashian, my nerves are worn very thin. There isn't any news about any other people in *People*; it should be called *"Person."* Thank goodness they are finally ready for me, but then of course, it takes a great deal of patience to have to sit there and have them give me a manicure while I am trying to find my phone somewhere in the depths of my purse to answer the urgent call from daughter asking me where I am, because she can't find her history book. I am sure I put it somewhere when I finished reading it, because, after all, academic history books are obviously one of my favorite things to read.

But the biggest test of patience comes when, after the soaking, and filing, and trimming, and clipping, and buffing, and polishing, you have to sit there, and wait for the blood to dry.

I think I've changed my mind about my New Year's Resolution. Instead of practicing to have more patience, I think I'll just give up getting manicures.

GOING THROUGH THE CHANGE

I'm going through the change and I hate it. It's that time that a lot of women look forward to with dread and anxiety, and I count myself among them.

Change is always hard. It wakes us up to the harsh fact that time is passing. Spring in particular seems to bring these things to light, and we have no choice but to change with the time. This change forces us to come face to face with our true selves, not how we wish to be seen, but with our reality. We might fool most of the people a lot of the time, we might even be able to fool ourselves for a while, by refusing to acknowledge the evidence, but the truth is there have been hints all along, we just choose to ignore them. However, the changing seasons of life eventually insist that we take an inventory of our selves, and then we have to admit that just maybe we are not exactly the person we present ourselves to be. The proof is right there, hidden in the dark recesses of our handbags. Sure, to the outside world we are smart, successful, competent women, and we have the power handbag to prove it. But, during the changing out of our winter handbags to the one we use for spring, our inner lives are forced out into the light, revealing us as the imposters we really are. I'm afraid that my handbag is like Dorian Gray's portrait, that the 'real' me will be discovered somewhere within all the contents of my purse.

It's hard to face the fact that, contrary to all outward appearances, I am really an unorganized mess of undone "To Do" lists, shopping lists, grocery lists, and library book lists, unused and out of date coupons, old tissues, loose pieces of gum with fuzz and hair stuck to them (cat and blonde), single arms to long lost pairs of glasses, a lens to lost sunglasses, old tubes of Chapstick, empty tubes of hand cream, a pair of those pedicure footies, a pair of my earplugs, a pair of my daughter's earplugs she asked me to hold for her, even though she has been away at college for this past year, something sharp that sticks my finger every time I lose my phone in there and shove my hand down in there to find it, broken pencils, and something black and sticky, probably a leaky pen. The thought of all this being a mirror of my life makes me start to feel all hot and panicked and then I remember the most important item of all, a little Xanax pill rolling around somewhere at the bottom of my purse. Although I have never actually had to use it, I panic if I can't find it, and I can't find it.

If it weren't for the time-honored tradition of changing out your handbag with the change of the seasons, I wouldn't have to face this uncharacteristic messy side of my self. I could just go on pretending that I am the same "has it all under control" woman that the outside of my handbag implies that I am. This year, though, I've finally had enough. I can feel a change coming on.

I relish the opportunity to turn over a new leaf, to once and for all become the woman I know I am- inside and out, the chance to Be The Handbag. I will first have to shop for a new handbag, because, after all, this is a new me, I can't very well go back to an old me handbag-but that is another story for another column. It's just a relicf to know that I will have a clean new bag to hold my clean and organized essentials for carrying my life around with me this spring. After going through a change that challenges us to take stock of things and offers the opportunity to gain more control of our lives, we come out a better version of ourselves, a new and improved version, sort of like a re-birth. So, I nervously dumped out all of the contents of my old life to sort things out, the good from the bad, and it was such a relief to find that little Xanax rolling around in there. I guess going through the change isn't going to be so bad after all.

THE EARLY SHOPPER

Oh, Boy! I am so excited! I just found the perfect gift for you and I can hardly wait till Christmas to give it to you. Wow! One down already, and it's only May!

I found this one-of-a-kind gift at a craft show and you and I are the only two people in the world who would appreciate it. I think of getting one for myself, too, but it was the only one left. Oh, well. I am ecstatic about how perfect this is for you, from me.

A couple of months later, when we are having lunch to catch up in July, I once again let it out that I already bought your Christmas gift. We vow not to let so much time get away until we see each other again. We'll talk soon!

September rolls around and I feel really good. I mean, I can proudly say that I have already started my Christmas shopping. I feel so relaxed going into the holiday gift-shopping season. No worries here! By the time November rolls around I feel that I am practically done with all of my shopping, after all, I started way back in the spring. I am not one of those slackers that waits around until the very last minute and have to get out into the Mall Madness, and the angry masses, that are pushing and shoving and begging and pleading and fighting over the very last coffee mug at the Hallmark store.

I feel sorry for all of those people who haven't even started their Christmas shopping and have to go out, at two o'clock in the morning Thanksgiving night, just to get some of their Christmas shopping done. I mean, hello, they knew Christmas was coming, all year long, just like it does every year. I am glad that I have already gotten most of my shopping done, so I can just relax, sleep in, and eat Thanksgiving leftovers all weekend. I feel so calm. I just have a couple of more things to get on my list, no big deal. I have plenty of time.

A couple of weeks later I wake up with a gnawing feeling, a vague sense of unease, but I can't quite put my finger on it. Throughout the next few days, that feeling begins to turn to dread, and then a sense of full-blown panic sets in. I look at the calendar and cannot believe that there are only seven days until Christmas! How the hell did this happen, I want to know?! Did Christmas get moved up this year? Was Thanksgiving late? Did they change Daylight Savings Time? OMG! I hope the stores are open extra late, don't they know people have to get their shopping done?!

Over the next seven days I spend hours driving and honking my horn, cursing under my breath, and wearily perusing websites late into the night in search of the perfect gifts for my family and friends. When, late one night, it suddenly dawns on me that you and I are going to get together this week for our annual Christmas gift swap. I am so excited! It's been six months, since we last got together back in July, too long. I remember that I already bought you a gift. I remember being excited about it. I vaguely remember that I got it at some craft show, but I can't quite remember what it was. I am panicked now, what was that gift I bought you? I am racking my brain trying to remember. I am ransacking my closets and drawers where I think I would put that perfect gift I bought for you. I don't see anything that reminds me of you. Just a lot of other forgotten gifts bought over the years.

What now? We are having brunch in the morning. Out of necessity I run to the Hallmark store and get you a coffee mug with a cat on it, because I know you love cats. And it can probably go with the one I gave you for your birthday-you'll have a set!

I come back home from our brunch with the coffee mug you gave me, with a Golden Retriever on it that you gave me, fix myself a cup of coffee in it, settle in by the fire and feel happy to have such a good friend as you, when I look up and see a little hand-made pottery cat and dog setting on the mantle, and think, that would have made such a perfect gift for you. I wonder where I got that?

"WOMAN GIVES BIRTH
TO 50 YEAR OLD!"
"It takes courage to grow up and become who you really are."
~ e. e. cummings

My 50th Birthday is right on my heels. That's getting on up there-and I'm afraid of heights! They say that getting older can be a real pain. I don't know about you, but the only pain I like is Champaign. But, thank goodness, I do have a high pain tolerance. I got it from my mother. My mom has a very high tolerance for pain; she said she lived with a pain in the ass for twenty-five years.

If the fifties are the middle ages, then I am having my own renaissance of sorts. As with other women of my Baby Boomer age, I am experiencing labor pains. It's hard enough birthing a new baby in your twenties, it's even harder giving birth to a fifty year old, but that feels exactly like what I am doing.

I guess I've really been going through the reinvention process for about the past seven years, although I didn't realize that was what I was doing until this year. I thought I was just killing some time while waiting on my kids to grow up. But, it turns out, that I was actually growing up, too. This birthday brings so many things into sharp focus, besides the obvious signs of aging. It brings clarity to the realization that NOW is the only time you have to live your life. For some this can be depressing. For me, it is liberating.

At least, it was, until I read an author interview in the *New York Times* about a new book that's out about turning fifty. I haven't read the book but the interview with the author made it sound like such a downer that it made me want to take some. The gist of it was that if you haven't reached your full potential by the time you are fifty then you are just out of luck. Sorry, she says, but if you are not rich and famous and fabulous and living your dream and thin by now, then you might as well just call it quits. I mean, after all, that is the whole goal, right? To hear her tell it, you might as well just go ahead and pull the plug-on your blog, your website, Facebook, Twitter, Pintrest, Instagram, photos, celebrations of any kind, this whole thing called your life, and pack up all your hopes and dreams and anti-aging products, dancing shoes and musical instruments and slip off quietly somewhere where nobody knows your name and nobody ever will. (By the way-this just seemed to apply to women)

No Fair! I am just getting started! I just found out that people were laughing at me! I can't help it that it didn't happen until I was almost fifty. I guess the joke is on me. Except, I am not laughing. And I really love to laugh. And I love to make other people laugh. I love that I write ideas that bring laughter into the world. I consider it to be a privilege. And I thought funny was funny no matter the age. I thought there was longevity in comedy. I guess I was wrong. Oh, would somebody tell Betty White? She didn't get that, either.

After being a stay-at-home-mom for the last twenty years I have been excited about stepping into my next stage of life. I really wish I had read this before I got my hopes up. I mean, I went and changed my name and everything. I even bought the new shoes to go with it!

Actually, one good thing about getting older is that you don't pay attention to the Negative Nellies and naysayers anymore. I am going to continue exploring my interests and how I might be able to give a bit of myself back to this world that gives us so much for which to be grateful every day. I am going to continue to offer a few more laughs into the world for whoever might be interested, after all, a laugh is meant to be shared, and the world could always use a little more of the happy sound of laughter in it, I think. Being a part of the last six months of the last of the Baby Boomer generation, I am a late Baby Bloomer, so I have a lot of catching up to do. But, all we ever really have is now, so, the way I look at it, now is always the right time to do whatever you want to do in life, to create the life you want.

That author might feel negative about being a baby boomer, and be ready to slip into a pair of safe, fuzzy slippers and say at least she tried, but this is one Boomer Babe who is looking forward to new adventures, high on life. After all, so many great adventures in life happen when you're high! It should be a great trip.

A NOTE ABOUT THE AUTHOR

Sunny Brown is a comedienne, entertainer, and writer, a recent "Empty Nester" and one of the last of the red, hot, baby boomers! In addition to writing and performing in her well received solo stage shows, she also writes and performs with the all female comedy/variety group *Feminine Hyjinx*, as well as writing her popular humor column, "The Glamorous Life", for *B-Metro Magazine*. She lives in her own little world and happily shares it with her husband, photographer Billy Brown, and their children's childhood pets that they have left behind; an old dog, an older cat, and an ancient tortoise.

Twitter: @itsreallysunny
Facebook: itsreallysunny
Instagram: itsreallysunny
www.itsreallysunny.com

Made in the USA
Middletown, DE
20 August 2015